DIVORCE POETRY

DIVORCE POETRY

Breaking Free

A Soul Healing Journey Through the Five Stages of Divorce

TAMARA MENDELSON

Copyright © 2015 Tamara Mendelson

All rights reserved.

ISBN: 1514383810
ISBN 13: 9781514383810
Library of Congress Control Number: 2015909873
Createspace Independent Publishing Platform
North Charleston, South Carolina

TABLE OF CONTENTS

Introduction · · · · · · · · · · · · · · · · ix

Chapter One: Breakdown · · · · · · · 1
   Rage Rising · · · · · · · · · · · · · · 3
   Silence · · · · · · · · · · · · · · · · · · 4
   Reflex · · · · · · · · · · · · · · · · · · · 5
   Irreconcilable Differences · · · · · 6
   Fire · 7
   A Squeaky Wheel· · · · · · · · · · · 8
   Brokenhearted · · · · · · · · · · · · · 9
   Every Word · · · · · · · · · · · · · · 10
   Sometimes · · · · · · · · · · · · · · · 11
   Storm Warning · · · · · · · · · · · 12
   The Fight · · · · · · · · · · · · · · · 13
   The Open Door· · · · · · · · · · · 14
   Trapped · · · · · · · · · · · · · · · · 15
   After the Firestorm · · · · · · · · 16
   Dinner for One · · · · · · · · · · · 17
   Listening · · · · · · · · · · · · · · · 18
   Ask · 19
   Peer Pressure · · · · · · · · · · · · · 20
   Glass Half Full· · · · · · · · · · · · 21

Chapter Two: Breakup · · · · · · · · 23
   Sentence · · · · · · · · · · · · · · · · 25
   Divorce in the Twenty-First
   Century · · · · · · · · · · · · · · · · 26
   Living a Lie · · · · · · · · · · · · · 27
   Casualties · · · · · · · · · · · · · · · 28
   Move On · · · · · · · · · · · · · · · 29
   Once upon a Time· · · · · · · · · 30
   Self-Portrait · · · · · · · · · · · · · 31
   It's Funny · · · · · · · · · · · · · · · 32
   The Other Side of the Bed · · · 33
   Hummingbird · · · · · · · · · · · · 34
   From Home to Home · · · · · · · 35
   Hear Me · · · · · · · · · · · · · · · · 36
   A Plan · · · · · · · · · · · · · · · · · 37
   Amen · · · · · · · · · · · · · · · · · · 38
   A Long, Dry Season· · · · · · · · 40
   For Show · · · · · · · · · · · · · · · 41

Chapter Three: Broken · · · · · · · · 43
   Early at the Beach · · · · · · · · 44
   Love Hurts · · · · · · · · · · · · · · 45

The Old Messages · · · · · · · · · 46
The New Rules · · · · · · · · · · · 47
You Must · · · · · · · · · · · · · · · · · 48
The Mind Forgets What the
Body Remembers · · · · · · · · · · · 49
All Growed Up · · · · · · · · · · · · · 50
Undertow · · · · · · · · · · · · · · · · · 51
Heart Stone · · · · · · · · · · · · · · · 52
Joint Custody · · · · · · · · · · · · · · 53
Silly Questions · · · · · · · · · · · · · 54
Habit · 55
No More Family Pictures · · · · 56
The Search for
Howland Island · · · · · · · · · · · · 57
The Stray We Saved · · · · · · · · 59
Kill the Critic · · · · · · · · · · · · · · 60
Lonely Wave · · · · · · · · · · · · · · 61

Chapter Four: Breakthrough · · · · 63
Marriage Investments · · · · · · · 65
Eventually Ever After · · · · · · · 66
Upsetting the Apple Cart · · · · 67
A Kiss to Carry
till Morning · · · · · · · · · · · · · · · 69
On Sex with the Ex · · · · · · · · · 70
Haiku · 71
Middle of the Night · · · · · · · · · 72
Crashing In · · · · · · · · · · · · · · · 73
Spring · 74
On the Wind · · · · · · · · · · · · · · 75
Sidewalk Chalk · · · · · · · · · · · · 76
Thoughts on Masturbation · · · 77
The Waves · · · · · · · · · · · · · · · · 78

Balloons · · · · · · · · · · · · · · · · · · 80
With Our Hearts, It Is
Not for Us to Say · · · · · · · · · · 83
Bashert · · · · · · · · · · · · · · · · · · · 84
The Path · · · · · · · · · · · · · · · · · · 85
Three More Candles · · · · · · · · 86
Gambling · · · · · · · · · · · · · · · · · 87
Happy Just to Dance · · · · · · · · 88
Cougar Town · · · · · · · · · · · · · · 89

Chapter Five: Break Free · · · · · · · 91
A Thorn · · · · · · · · · · · · · · · · · · 93
Yawning and Stretching · · · · · 94
Not Finished · · · · · · · · · · · · · · 95
Not So Hard to Find · · · · · · · · 96
Someone Else's Child · · · · · · · 97
E-Mail from a Man · · · · · · · · · 98
How Can I Pretend? · · · · · · · · 99
A Moment · · · · · · · · · · · · · · · 100
First Light · · · · · · · · · · · · · · · 101
How to Teach a
Nine-Year-Old How to
Dribble a Basketball · · · · · · · 102
I Dreamed of the House
We Used to Share · · · · · · · · · 104
In My Dreams · · · · · · · · · · · · 105
Melancholy Hearts · · · · · · · · 106
Nicole's Horse · · · · · · · · · · · · 107
My Rock? · · · · · · · · · · · · · · · · 108
Salt and Pepper · · · · · · · · · · · 109
The First Rain · · · · · · · · · · · · 110
A Different Kind of
Good-Bye · · · · · · · · · · · · · · · · 111

The House · · · · · · · · · · · · · · · 113	Till Death · · · · · · · · · · · · · · · 119
A Late-in-Life Love Song · · · 114	Today · · · · · · · · · · · · · · · · · · 120
Because · · · · · · · · · · · · · · · · · 115	Wonderment · · · · · · · · · · · · 121
Just Not as Husband and Wife · · · · · · · · · · · · · · · · 116	Quiet · · · · · · · · · · · · · · · · · · · 122
Lips · 117	Broken Free · · · · · · · · · · · · · 123
Self-Acceptance · · · · · · · · · · 118	About the Author · · · · · · · · · · · 125

INTRODUCTION

Fifty percent of married couples will go through the heartbreaking process of ending their marriage. A surprising fact is that a full 25 percent, one in four, of American divorces involves baby boomers, couples over fifty years of age. It's a fast-growing divorce trend that people are writing about in the *Los Angeles Times*, *Huffington Post*, and *Wall Street Journal*, and talking about on NPR, CNN, and Fox News. In fact, this trend even has a name: the "gray divorce."

One researcher explained the phenomenon of empty nesters looking forward this way: "In the past, many people simply didn't live long enough to reach the 40-year itch. You can't divorce if you're dead." Another quipped, "Turns out that Tipper and Al Gore, and Maria Shiver and Arnold Schwarzenegger are examples of the reshaping of the contours of divorce in America."

Divorce is the second most stressful event in a person's life, after the death of a loved one. But to be fair, the death of a marriage is still death. It is also the destruction of a family unit and, in many cases like mine, the loss of self-worth. Add children and finances into the mix and divorce is a heartbreaking mess.

Alas, joining the ranks of Tipper and Maria doesn't make divorce more socially acceptable. Divorce is, and always will be, painful, messy, sad, and debilitating. Why? Because divorce sucks.

I was never getting divorced. Marriage was forever. But forever turned out to be seventeen years. I'm not sure exactly when the bottom started to fall out; it didn't happen at once. At some point, we stopped treating each other with the respect and compassion required for a lifetime together. Polite held for a while, but we were stuck on a slow simmer. Things just got blacker and uglier. Picking on each other over petty things transformed itself into bickering. But for the kids, we tried to fly the mortally wounded plane. The turbulence and smoke became intolerable.

My decision to bail took years. Quitting was not in me. All the while, losing altitude, we endured the gut-wrenching finale. We knew what was coming.

Well, I knew what was coming; he ignored it. But like a head-on collision, the shock and damage were no less terrifying just because you might have seen them coming. I overcompensated by trying to be superparent to our teenage kids. Yet, I couldn't eat or sleep. Relief and regret went hand in hand. Most frightening was not knowing who I would be if alone.

Truth be told, this was all the more difficult because my profound sadness was not the result of any spectacular blunder by my husband. He didn't beat me. He was a good father (although much better as a single father). I don't think he cheated, either. We lived comfortably, too. But we all have the right to happiness in a marriage. My preservation instinct pounded on me to distance myself from the pain, even if divorce was inconceivable to friends and family.

No, he never raised a hand to me, but he was still my emotional terrorist. From the outside, we were the model family, but from where I laid my head, without splitting from him, I would have been stereotypically "settling" for decades more of a loveless marriage, at best—a fate reserved for past generations, couples whose decay and sad complacency were preferable to embarrassment, stigmatism, and starting over.

It didn't help much that intimacy had vanished a decade before, replaced by fleeting blue-pill sex by the numbers. Now, edging toward fifty, I grasped in my heart that this bird was cooked.

I started writing poetry again—a lifelong passion that I sacrificed during my marriage, which should have been a clue to having lost my identity. I started to recognize myself again in my writing. I was suddenly able to heal by painfully conversing with myself through verse.

Our marriage counselor, who thought me a troublemaker, was far more interested in the color of my shoes than the agony in my soul. My oblivious husband charmed the wrong woman in the room. He was predictably inculpable. His pseudo-truth mantra was, "I am not responsible for your happiness." As his spouse, not his business partner, I believed that happiness was our most basic responsibility to each other; as a soon-to-be ex-wife, I finally comprehended that my soon-to-be ex-husband neither understood nor undertook this mutual commitment.

I continued writing. It was far more effective.

While still in denial, with my glass-half-full perspective, I did not realize that my "mundane," not *Burning Bed*, divorce process was almost universal. Everyone is torn apart. When I started to show my poetry, I often heard, "That's exactly how I felt."

Divorce isn't like ripping off a Band-Aid; it's not instantaneous, briefly painful and then painless. The agonizing decision may take years, and every step is a potential minefield. All the while, time is slipping away—time in life. After, like a war wound, it leaves a scar or limp. There are whispers and shunning and questions of fault, none of which is anyone's business. It's the scarlet letter "D" that adorns us, whether we like it or not.

From the outside, we were perfect. We had teenage children, enjoyed challenging and creative careers, threw great parties, and had an enviable life by most standards. Ironically, the outside didn't much match the inside. The dissonance was volcanic for me. The distant, closing siren blocked out everything else. Even the occasional good stuff was lost. And the ringing stayed with me, even after the emergency vehicle was long gone. Divorce tinnitus.

Is a civilized divorce possible? I had hoped so. However, there is nothing civilized about tearing a family asunder. What was ours suddenly became his or mine, dividing friends, families, the silverware, and the dog.

Couples fight. I got that. But for us, there were no resolutions, no makeup sex. There was neither compromise nor resolution. Emotionally, we only shared an accelerating deterioration in our crumbling status quo. At one point, my bubbly personality was corked. I was not allowed an opinion. I was bitter, angry, and defeated. All I ever really wanted was to be on the same team, but we weren't in the same ballpark. My soul ached. The stress transformed itself into stomach acid culminating in a couple of evenings in the ER.

When we were both working hard at keeping this plane aloft, I remember going away for the weekend, just the two of us. I was looking forward to reconnecting, to connection. Vacations were always good for us. He single-mindedly booked a place that was my tenth choice of ten, but I was going to be pleasant, even if it killed me. Although we obviously had a room, we ended up spending every minute with a group. My husband chatted with the chef for most of the meal. I suggested that my husband return to the table. He didn't. I got up a second time and stood by him as he continued his chat with the chef. After being ignored for a few more minutes, I returned to the table alone for the rest of the meal. I was upset, but didn't want to spoil the weekend—or the metaphor. We got up early the next morning for an intimate breakfast. Intimacy was what I craved. What I got was breakfast with the same group. This was his intimacy. I was ready to go home to our kids. I said very clearly and calmly that I would like to go home. He said no. And I accepted his no. Can you imagine? I had money in my wallet to get a cab. However, there is no "I" in "team" and I was a slow learner.

We had grown apart, grown to like different things, grown into different people. Maybe we always had liked different things. More to the point, maybe I simply stopped pretending to like the things he liked. We found pleasure in different people. What was clear under our chuppah was that we were from different countries and cultures; what was clear in the end was that we never shared goals or dreams. His goals were measured by financial and social success, while mine were centered on family and happiness. His point of view, which was somewhat culturally driven, was that financial and social success were the only ways to achieve family happiness. My point of view by the end was that I would trade all the money and parties in the world for ten minutes of emotional intimacy.

And as long as all the cards are on the table, I married an Israeli war veteran who was my senior on his second marital tour of duty. We did not necessarily get married for all the right reasons, but we had enough in common to think it would work. Like every marriage, we started with love and sex and a bright future. However, he always believed that he knew what was best for me and for us, and I generally deferred to him for an equal measure of right and wrong reasons. On the other hand, I thought I could fix him, too, which was probably no less frustrating to him, and is no better.

It was November 2009. We were attending a large extravagant wedding, a lovely soiree with soft lighting and white flowers and the great joy of a blessed beginning. I had a knot in my stomach the size of the bridal bouquet. A sense of dread that had been growing steadily for years, but was becoming impossible to deny, was now taking center stage. While watching their postnuptial slideshow featuring the skydiving marriage proposal, the young couple gazed blissfully into each other's eyes. I wiped my cheeks and realized that I would never have that with this husband of mine. Indeed, it occurred to me that perhaps I had never had it with him. Crushing sorrow overcame me. I wished the bride and groom well, grabbed my children, and fled the building. Two weeks later, we were in therapy. I began writing again. I went out and got a master's degree in creative writing and English literature. The floodgates were opening.

Ten months later, we were no longer living in the same house. Within the year, we were divorced. He was and is a very good man, not a villain in any way. Surprisingly, he is now a much better father and friend than he was as a husband. We simply weren't meant to be together and, ultimately, we both knew it. This book of about a hundred poems reflects my journey.

Psychiatrist Elisabeth Kübler-Ross, in her 1969 book, *On Death and Dying*, was inspired by her work with terminally ill patients. She famously broke grieving down into five stages: denial, anger, bargaining, depression, and acceptance. Borrowing from her work, I have broken down my journey—and this book—into the following chapters/stages:

Breakdown   *Breakup*   *Broken*   *Breakthrough*   *Break Free*

Thank you for picking up this book. I hope that you never have to live through divorce. If you do, I hope that your experience is at least a tiny bit more peaceful than mine was. If you already experienced divorce, I hope that we have communicated, like survivors of different plane crashes onto the same island.

Tamara Mendelson, 2015

CHAPTER ONE: BREAKDOWN

Breakdown is the beginning of the end, the fraying at the edges of your kid's 12-year-old blankie. Little cracks and real problems start wheezing, disrupting communication. That noise is not yet even a cough, let alone death rumble, but it is persistent enough to start shifting off the axis, just slightly. It feels like running with a pebble in your shoe, or dust in your lungs. You run a while, as you can't be bothered to stop. After more irritation, what was once bearable becomes painful. You stop, catch your breath and take off the shoe, coughing and shaking out the pebble, hopping around adjusting your sock, and probably finishing the run. But, nothing feels right or the same. Still chaffing and irritating, you stop and you check again, examining the irritant. You sit down and pulling off your sock and, skimming your fingertips all over your foot, other abrasions are discovered. Perhaps it is an old bruise. But, you put back on your sock and shoe, cough into your sleeve, and start out again slower, more tentative, off balance and uncomfortable in your own shoes, skin or home.

Maybe you think about seeing your local clergy or therapist to try to get back on track. Everyone has problems. And you begin to notice other things, behaviors that you have ignored – yours and his. Maybe you don't even like running.

It's the doubt that seeps in during the Breakdown. The seepage is terrifying. You tried to ignore the pebble as long as possible, but it's niggling and burning. Then, all of a sudden you pay attention. Everything changes. The pebble isn't there anymore, but the damage is done. The memory of being an "I", not a "we", replaces the pebble. Things start to fall apart. Piece by piece, you don't want to hold it together anymore – or you can't hold it together – and you begin the Breakdown.

RAGE RISING

Rage rises off you
in shimmering waves
disturbing the air,
with movement and vibration,
nothing really moves.

It dissipates,
spreading out and clinging to
everything.

And circles like a cyclone
black and thick,
wiping out the sun.

And when you are sure
everyone is swept up
you step away.

SILENCE

Silence is louder than lightning.
There is no flash to blind.
The nothingness of an echo
that is swallowed by a chasm.
Words left unsaid stuck in my mouth,
swallowed bitter and whole.
And rest in my belly covering
anger after all covers sadness,
no light in the darkness,
no sound.

REFLEX

The words come like the reflex of a spring
Bound tight and compressed until let go
And I am sure they don't mean a thing
As they bounce back and forth an ebb and flow.

Sometimes I have felt the metal sting
As it snaps my unprotected skin
And I step away just outside of reach
Waiting for the spring to be sprung again.

IRRECONCILABLE DIFFERENCES

I quiver under the glare of disapproval.
There may as well be bars, a lock and key.
To reinvent myself anew again and again,
each version meant to please.

And I do not recognize the parts
in the darkness scattered about me,
like decaying leaves,
disconnected pieces of the whole.

Whatever form I take, twisted and unnatural,
shallow toxic breaths to sustain me.
And I swallow the damp dark air
again I am met with deep sighs and frustrations,
lash and condemnation.
And I leak all over from the bits.
Not fashioned back into the whole.

The cell gets smaller and the floor
underneath unstable.
I strain to stay upright and unmoved,
my toes carve grooves into stone.
As I hang on hopelessly
under the burden of shifting winds
and changing tides, not quite whole.

Damp dark air heavy with bitterness,
and longing greets me with the sun.

FIRE

Sadness falls
like a dark curtain blocking out the light.
The ache spreads like a brush fire,
consuming, ravaging everything in its path.
Unstoppable.
Until the wind changes,
or there is nothing left to burn.
And coals smolder white-hot ash
and then the fire dies,
for lack of fuel,
leaving behind blackened earth,
and a hole where once was life
now deadened air.

A SQUEAKY WHEEL

He still believes that I am not a squeaky
wheel I asked him once why I was last in line
"It is the squeaky wheel that gets the grease"
He replied, "You are the one I do not have to worry about."
I did not understand at first that worrying
about me was different somehow,
connected to worrying about himself.
A weather gauge for mental health
and I became the one who didn't squeak
my soft smooth calls unanswered,
I swallowed my questions and looked
other places for other answers.
And learned to be something else
I was strong when I did not feel
strong and brave when I was afraid
and smiled when I thought my heart would break
and then he was OK, with me being OK.
He loved me unconditionally when I was able,
not when I was cracked or broken or fearful.
I looked like I knew exactly what I was doing,
I told myself acting OK was part of the routine
Eventually, I would come to believe it, too.
Pulling all the broken pieces back together
like a shattered mirror, almost whole, resurrected
there are always a few shards missing.

BROKENHEARTED

The pain has finally split my heart in two
Halves that will not be again together
The break was ragged want to seal anew
Some are lost to me now and forever

My ravaged heart still beats a different time
I do not recognize the new-formed flow
Why did I not see the heart was mine?
Concentrating on my breathing deep and slow

And with two pieces I will now go on The
path unknown to me and so unclear
The sore muscles from overuse are strong
The worst is past and nothing left to fear

Although I cannot see my way ahead
Hearts are blind; I'll use my eyes instead.

EVERY WORD

I will remember every word you say
Take care with the things that fall from your lips
Uttered in abandon hang in the air
Little reminders of your fall from grace
And what you think you have you may not

SOMETIMES

I don't know where you go when you leave.
Right here in my arms and you are far away.
Your breathing matches my own,
your eyes open
and focused
but not on me.
On something else or somewhere else
I cannot see.
Where you must get all the things you
want, and everything you need,
and none of the heartache or pain,
that I see in your eyes when
you are not looking at me.

STORM WARNING

The winter waves that pound the shore,
do not quite drown the rotors' roar.
Helicopters patrol the beach,
Like predators at low tide.
The sky is blue the water warm
black flags whip about,
warning of dangers just below the waves.
Predictions of violent storms,
and there are no lifeguards
on this side of the beach.

THE FIGHT

A breath caught in my chest an ache so sharp,
bleary-eyed for a moment I cannot see
I should not have let the words get past my lips
Now it is too late to let things be.

The harm is done the wound laid bare,
shocked by the brightness of the blood.
As if I had plunged a dagger sharp and rare.
And now the sound, a dull and weakened thud.

In my heart I cannot speak your name,
words that harm, I did not take care.
Things will never ever be the same,
I cannot stop the bleeding, which seems fair.

THE OPEN DOOR

Can I forgive you and not forgive myself?
The cell door is open,
and I bounce back and forth inside the bars
unable or unwilling to set myself free.
Aiming again and again for the opening,
To be out in the air unfettered and alone,
I cannot cross the threshold,
a chain around my heart.
The bars cast a golden glow,
the cage so well appointed,
thick lush carpets cover the cold floor.
Colors woven together like blood, flesh, and bone.
Linen drapery filters out the harshest light,
pillows fluffed from the purest down,
from the live coats of geese.
And here I remain fattened and afraid and
angry unable to forgive, unable to forget.
Unable and unwilling to set myself free.

TRAPPED

Trapped by five thousand years of history
Tears disappear into the sand
Bound by promises never made
Growing old and dry like the earth
Parched and cracked
No longer able to sustain life
Flash floods rob nutrients and soil
After many rainless seasons
Nothing left to hang on to
Dust swirls through fingers
Blinds and chokes
Gates stand sentinel to pockmarks
of old battles and new wars
Always a new war
I want to throw off the shackles
of one hundred generations of responsibility
Return to the rain-soaked freshness of home.
Young, green, alive, and free.

AFTER THE FIRESTORM

Anger feeds the raging inferno consuming everything
Until the wind shifts and there is nothing left to burn
As rage cools, no constant fuel to sustain the fire
White coals turn to ash spiraling and circling on the wind
The ground is dark and deadened broken shifting.
Bare open wounds choke and sputter heaving.

Heat waves settle and rain begins like tears washing the charred earth,
Steam rises and blankets the sky like the beginning.
Sadness descends and fear bubbles up through the ash and smoke,
only time will heal this parched and decimated ground.
And after a time, some time, four seasons or eight or more,
a tiny brave green stalk of life will push up toward the sun.

DINNER FOR ONE

Sitting at the table watching the ice in your water glass melt.
Talking and laughing swirling all around me, I am untouched.
Flickering tea lights, soft and romantic. Music inviting and familiar.
Breathing deeply I take another piece of bread and try to eat slowly,
giving me something to do with my hands and passing the time.
Getting sympathetic looks from the waiter topping off my glass.
Twisting the bottle not a drop of the deep red liquid lost.
Wondering how I got to this point of aloneness and invisibility?
Ribbing from the rest of our companions they too are wondering
Waiting for you to realize you left me alone, again.
Knowing it makes little difference as you are getting what you need.
Nothing to do with me, the fact only compounds my embarrassment.
Warranting not even an afterthought. Our entrées arrive.
Returning briefly you whisk your plate away to the bar.
Continuing your conversation with the chef you just met.
Walking to the corner of the bar, I standing quietly,
touching your arm lightly reminding you I am here.
Trying to coax you back to the table, our friends and me.
Turning your shoulder away I nod to the chef and return to the table.
Understanding by gesture that nothing has changed.
Glistening condensation beads down the side of your water glass,
looking like tears. The waiter approaches with more wine.

LISTENING

Your voice throbbed with pain,
No pause to slow the rhythm.
I just listened with my whole heart,
My understanding was moot.
It is your trauma and indecision?
The cut deep and will take great care
to stanch the heavy bleeding,
then to stitch the wound tightly.
Too much blood lost,
A transfusion, a necessity.
My blood is your blood.
Then perhaps the healing might begin,
when the injured tissues are treated with time and care.
Not left alone, ignored and abandoned to fester,
an infection or relapse could prove fatal.
For recovery is uncertain.

ASK

Help is on the way
You need to know what to ask
When it gets to you

PEER PRESSURE

Everyone else does
Is not a reason to do,
Anything ever.

GLASS HALF FULL

I see the golden leaves fallen after the rain,
You see a pile of rubbish that needs cleaning.
I see the tall strong sugarcane grown over the fence,
You see overgrown stocks leaning into the neighbor's yard.

I see a house full of love, laughter and clutter.
You see disorder, disarray and idleness.
I see something that can begin again tomorrow,
You see something that agitates you into restlessness.

I do not need to control everything I can.
You need order and things always in their places.
There is no place to just be in our house,
No place to just be with you, no place at all.

CHAPTER TWO: BREAKUP

Breakups are seldom sudden. They encompass both emotional and physical separation. We try to make up and rejoin, but separate again and again. Objects begin to be points of contention in an almost-covert negotiation. Money might have been tight before, but now you are impossibly stretched. Fear is a constant companion, while change swirls around everyone and everything. The dissolving relationship creates a transition as the new reality is born. You face who you are without your spouse, where you're going, and multitudes of emergencies along the way. Children, friends, and family react and overreact. Emotional tornados whip up pain along their paths.

Struggling with new responsibilities on the outside, one must simultaneously manage all of the fear, anger, and sadness raging inside. Friends and family call out to be reassured, yet you are in no condition to reassure anyone.

Divorce is a difficult enough concept for adults, but try to explain it to a child. Are they being abandoned? Why do they have to suffer? Is it their fault? Trying to maintain some small piece of family when you can't stand even to be in the same room as your spouse is like gardening in one of those tornados. Yet, the superhuman strength to pull this off is dwarfed by the desire to expose your feelings about their other parent. But you cannot because they still have to live, at least part time, with your spouse, even if you can escape. Children are smart. They watch for any cracks in the resolve. They know from television and movies and from their friends in "broken homes" what is in play. They get angry, pleading for the status quo. The pressure can bring even the strongest of us to tears, self-doubt, and despair.

When that twister is bearing down and you cannot quite get the shutter door closed, spending time with old friends from before the marriage can help reset the emotional compass. self-worth, and confidence. But, for now, it's going to get worse before it gets better. And it's advisable to hunker down in your emotional safe room for when the breakdown becomes broken.

SENTENCE

Single seems like a sentence if divorce is the crime.
Nothing stolen, except for life and time.

DIVORCE IN THE TWENTY-FIRST CENTURY

Forever and ever
It was never my intention to hurt you
In a fight to survive I chose me.
Our proudest accomplishments,
those being we brought into existence.
To them safe and sound and happy,
Is our main responsibility.

He said: I am not responsible for your happiness.
She said: Your happiness was more important than my life and even that was not enough.

LIVING A LIE

Is it still a lie?
If you are the only one who knows the truth?
The truth that hides behind a smile
and is buried beneath a cascade of laughter
Is it the truth that wakes you up at 4:00 a.m.?
In a cold sweat with heart palpitations?
When the world sleeps
And you can't breathe
Is it still a lie?
If it isn't true all the time
just most, when the world is so quiet,
your heartbeat pounds in your ears.
So you keep moving,
and doing and rushing,
distracting from the ache,
you carry in your chest like a stone.
Is it still a lie?
If years go by and the ache becomes
part of every day and you don't remember
how to take a deep breath.
And you don't remember what you wanted
in the first place.
And your eyes are always sad,
even when you are laughing and lying.

CASUALTIES

The pain in your voice
cuts like a knife,
the blade is sharp and swift,
the wound a clean, thin red line
until the blood overflows,
and cannot be stanched,
by the pressure of words,
or hands or soothing murmurings,
and I wonder if I add to the conflict,
as you block body blows
with your duty-bound hands bound,
honor and responsibilities.

And the fighting continues
unabated by a cease-fire
and late-night secret conferences,
then ever-smiling photographs,
journalists chronicling
the bizarre events
for all time.
And I wonder
if dawn on the horizon
will bring relief for
the casualties of the heart,
or the battle will go on
indefinitely.
Until someone cries,
"Enough."

MOVE ON

You asked me if I am disappointed.
No, not disappointed,
Not as a child who learns
he cannot fly.
But is grounded
Like other earthbound animals.

You mean to ask, disappointed with you.
Not the disappointment that comes
at the end of a life, with a dream
of love never realized. Or the sadness
that comes when there is no time
to say good-bye.

If I am disappointed,
It is the disappointment
that comes from a picnic
rained out, a darkened sky.
When there is no hope
of a rainbow.

And yes, disappointed like
expectations of the hungry,
when there is no more,
turned out and away,
back to the cold streets,
where one must move on
or slowly starve.

ONCE UPON A TIME

I do not know,
if another magic kiss,
might turn me back into a frog.
And then I will have to return
to life in the lily pond.
Hopping aimlessly from pad to pad
using my tongue to catch flies.
No one wants to caress a slimy frog,
and I won't even have lips
to remember the tingle
that lingers after
a magic kiss.

SELF-PORTRAIT

The second tree planted, one from the right.
Strong roots, straight branches, weight-bearing limbs.
No shoring up or staking down,
and no special handling.
The others in the garden need pruning
and constant care,
as by a weaker constitution,
and not too much sunlight.
They are the same, but no great expectations,
beyond the basic living year to year,
sharing nothing, blooming seldom,
rest shelter, shade granting, wind blocking.

The soil is turned over and replaced.
The squeaky wheel, the ailing trees,
nutrients added to the earth.
Around the garden, the bag is empty,
the ground half done, it is enough,
for this tree has grown and done without
constant attention or care.
A house is built in the stocky base,
where the largest branches are attached.
Steps as rungs are made by hatchet
small injuries and scars, a tire swing hung.
The tree has a long gash above the root,
an old wound just below the ground,
from which it quietly weeps.

IT'S FUNNY

It's funny now that I want you I can't have you
Never thought of us together and here we are
You aren't mine and never will be
And now I want you and it's funny.
In a sad ironic sort of way maybe that's why
It works so well. No past and no future.
Just the now? Never thought now
would be enough, now not sure.
This must be what love feels like,
the heartbeat, the fight or flight.
Nothing about any of this is funny.
But it's real and it must be love.

THE OTHER SIDE OF THE BED

I can't sleep there on the left
It's always been my side on the right
Not the left nearest the window
The right side next to the door.
I can sleep in the middle now,
with the light and the television on.
No earphones or earplugs required and still,
I cannot sleep on the other side,
alone in this big bed.

HUMMINGBIRD

Ruby-headed hummingbird
clicks at me
from the other side
of the plate glass
window
the feeder frozen
his sharp beak
cannot break
the thin ice
to the sugar water
below

Why has he not
traveled south
to more temperate climes?
Beating his black
wings so swiftly
I cannot
see them
flutter
Is that how he stays warm?

FROM HOME TO HOME

Here is your house with
your language and six
generations buried in the backyard.

I walk alone through
doorways dizzy, unable
to get my balance.

My things out of place.
It is too hot
to sit on plastic furniture.
Slick skin sticking to the legs,
gulping wet air.
Sometimes the rain on the roof
sounds like familiar footsteps.

My people are not here, my soul
is split geographically,
across oceans and continents.

Where are the songs
from my childhood?
You don't know them
I can't sing alone.

The phone line, voices echo
like a deep-sea diver,
oxygen tanks on my back,
breathing through water.

HEAR ME

You will not raise your hand
to me again.
There is no more bend,
and it has been
too long since I
have seen the sky.

Wounded as you are,
I have forgiven you.
Our children are frightened
and for that you have
given up the privilege
of being part of us.

Where we are going
is quiet and safe.
You cannot follow.
There are no more chances.
Sorry means nothing,
and you will be alone.

A PLAN

There is not a book to tell you how to break up a home.
To separate property yes, legal, fair and binding.
How to tell the children but what about after that?
There is no graceful way to exit from a contract,
when love and promise give way to sadness and despair.
And friends dart and take the breakup personally.
To fight or flee to hide away the pain and smile as if
my world has not fallen apart and free advice
from those with no experience are only judgments.

AMEN

When the shofar is sounded
Ancient primitive and raw,
it is the soul crying out
There is no sense in comparing,
All human pain is the same.
And we all ache, deep and wounded.
And we learn and we grow,
And we love and we hurt,
And then what we know is only what we know,
until someone shows us or we learn or we see
differently and then we know better,
and we do the best we can,
and there is no reason to compare,
we all carry the same agony from the beginning.
And we all have to figure out a way to go on.
No one gets through this life without pain.
Unless one doesn't really live a life at all,
A life…
Without joy
Without hope
Without love
Without laughter
Without disappointment
Without heartache
Without failure
Without tragedy
Without triumph
Without a little peace
Without pain

so-deep-down-you-can't-take-another-breath kind of pain
And then you inhale just a little, almost by accident
as a reflex, and your lungs know what to do even if the
rest of you does not
Hearts keep beating, and one foot in front of the other,
no perfection, just perseverance and the joy of living
one breath at a time.
Amen

A LONG, DRY SEASON

Is the breeze cooler? A tall shadow passes.
A fluffy, harmless cloud of no help.
Fingers lightly brushing across a pale cheek,
blush rising quickly and then disappearing.
Never there at all or just a little heat.
Lonely lips hold fast the taste of a kiss,
vine-ripened sweetness drips, the chin is dry.
A memory of moisture, wetness dew.
Tomorrow the sun will rise again,
hot and unforgiving by midday.
Ceiling fan whirs imitating wind.
Perspiration beads, parched shallow breath.
Sheets twisted damp. And if I sleep, if I sleep.
I will dream of rain.

FOR SHOW

I watch you cater to the people you care least about
As long as it looks like a success. Basking in their praise.
As long as everything looks good from the outside,
happiness is harder to see and not as measurable.
Not like a win or handmade dishes from Italy,
or being called everyone's favorite host,
in a house that is great for entertaining.
As we prepare for another show to begin,
that feeling grabs hold of my stomach,
I want to run screaming from the room, "Enough!"
Wound so tight I cannot unclench my fingers.
Bile surges into my throat and I swallow fire again.
Burning behind the smile and I play along and die a little.
This is not what love is supposed to feel like.

CHAPTER THREE: BROKEN

Your heart is broken. It is no consolation knowing that, ultimately, divorce is for the best. It is hard to breathe. Depression, guilt, and sadness are pervasive. Getting out of bed never seems like a good idea. Every day is a huge effort, believing that the sadness will destroy you, drown you in blackness, and suffocate your very soul.

A black mood. Friends and family think that socializing might lighten things up. Being the only one without a partner—even if you don't want a partner—makes dinner parties emotional crime scenes. The favorite question, even before the ink is dry, is, "Who are you dating?" They chatter, "I have a divorced friend who is coming tonight who will be perfect for you." You play along, asking, "Really? What do we have in common?" You wait for it, like bile after a heave: "You are both divorced."

EARLY AT THE BEACH

The sand is not yet warm from the morning sun
In a matter of hours it will be too hot to walk barefoot
For now, I sit at the edge where the water meets the shore
White cotton shirt stretched over my knees, in my shell.
Just my toes wriggle deeper into the damp, dark world.
And I am rocking to and fro with the rhythm of the tide.
A small brown crab scrambles sideways over my toes.
I laugh out loud and scare a seagull into flight.
It is quiet again just the lapping of the waves,
and I am listening for your voice to echo my laughter,
floating on the currents of air out to sea.

LOVE HURTS

When it's real and good and fluid
The ebb and flow of expectations
Disappointment felt deep in my chest
Hollow, empty, alone and dark

The waning of the moon
Cycles and arches across the heavens
I strain against them all
Impossible and yet I fight blindly

Struggling against the power of time
There is no triumphant rebel yell
Winning is futile and in the effort
Only grieving and loss

In my shattered state I wonder
Why I fight at all but hope
Is a wonder as big as the sky
As deep as the ocean

And I watch the tide
For a time and then you smile
the sun breaks through the clouds
The tempest tossed now still

THE OLD MESSAGES

It hasn't been that long and yet
Is it possible to forget?
Everything you promised
And everything you said?

I try to be brave and yet
the nagging feeling in my chest
does not allow me to rest
and I wonder how long?

I counted on the things you said.
You don't remember and yet
my decisions were based
on your answers now erased.

And the feeling of betrayal does not
go away the words you didn't mean
the things you didn't say.
My battered heart will break again.

And I will howl a wounded cry
An endless hurt and I know why.

THE NEW RULES

Your voice betrays more than your words admit.
The pain I am familiar with in kind.
Your heart, to cease its beating, and then quit.
To see her face hard fast resolve resigns.
The passion is now cloistered clean away,
trying to follow all the new-made rules.
Uncomfortable the role you now must play,
To persevere and then to play thefool.
Fools love too easily and so complete.
At the mercy of their object desired,
to choose love and be carefully discreet.
To ignore the muse that so deeply inspires.

The question is not how the fool be judged,
is it better to love than to be loved?

YOU MUST

You must go out
into the light
and feel the sun
upon your face.
This house is full
of rotting things
and age and death.

You must go out
and breathe the air
and fill your lungs
with living things.
This house is full
decayed and dying
the last breath.

You must go out
and join the living
dance barefoot
in rich moist soil
and fill your hair
with fresh-picked flowers
and scatter seeds
of spring, to live.

THE MIND FORGETS WHAT THE BODY REMEMBERS

The mind forgets what the body cannot
Wounds heal and scars fade but not the thirst
Recovery slow with pain sharp and hot

A smile shows the onlookers what is not
Smoldering white just below the surface
The mind forgets what the body cannot

Dreams make the body whole false thought
Battle scars no feeling numb and cursed
Recovery slow with pain sharp and hot

Passion is another touch that's fraught
With ghosts of touch and spirits' fingers nursed
The mind forgets what the body cannot

Traumas of the flesh the mind tries to blot
Memory tricks, potions, pills rehearsed
Recovery slow with pain sharp and hot

The cold sweat that wakes a tortured thought
In darkness shivering the body injured still
The mind forgets what the body cannot
Recovery slow with pain sharp and hot

ALL GROWED UP

Being all growed up is being who you are really deep down
no matter what anyone else says or does or thinks.
This is one of the hardest things to learn and the easiest thing to be.

UNDERTOW

Under the covers,
eyes squeezed tight,
days and nights the same.
The common thread, pain.
Herculean effort to get out of bed,
climbing to the summit of Kilimanjaro.
To put my feet on the floor.
The weight in my chest
where my heart used to be,
denies deep breaths.
Struggling against the current.
Swimming without the energy or oxygen to fight.
Circles upon circles swirling undertow,
dragging me down to the center,
stronger than gravity.
I can only tread water for so long.

HEART STONE

The size of a fist
lodged between my ribs.
Bruised from within,
a hollowed-out place,
I worked hard to clear.
Filled up again.
The heft of a stone,
painful and familiar, it tries to settle.
Interfering with my breathing.

It comes on suddenly.
Like switching off a light.
A word said, a deed undone,
Sidelined or rejected in shadow,
Vicious whispers and blame.

Or comes slow like a memory,
heavier with each expulsion.
It must be expelled again now.
Before gravity and history,
settle it with permanency.

JOINT CUSTODY

Like a ghost I walk the house at night,
checking and rechecking the locks and doors.
Illumination unnecessary, my feet have mapped every inch
with fingertips I have smoothed the walls,
On many nights of noiseless wanderings.
Floating in and out of rooms hunting
for a sign of something stirring.
Cats like statues sleep unmoved.
The beds are made and empty, quiet
They are waiting, too, for the life to return.
Toys on shelves abandoned memories inlaid
deeper with each silent breath.
Shoes lined up like soldiers.
I look down at my bare feet,
and the pale glow startles me.

SILLY QUESTIONS

When I was young the uncles asked about my boyfriends,
As they held me too close and pet my cheeks and
damped dreams with old men's breath.
Never asked about my hopes and my desires.
They asked my brother about school and me about dances
Not politics, Plato and poetry from my soul.
They told me I was pretty and why did I need to worry?
About the world, and big ideas and satisfying work.
I was married for a long time and then divorced.
And now they ask about my children, and my boyfriends
comment on the size of my jeans and why not just color my hair?
Not freedom, not longing and desire. The search of self.
And after fifty years, for it finally to be enough, just being me.
The aunties are the ones I carry in my heart.
The ones who didn't concern themselves with silly questions.
And quietly conquered the world.

HABIT

Has it been working?
If not, then tear it all down
And start again fresh

NO MORE FAMILY PICTURES

No more family pictures
Pieces are missing.
The original six that grew to ten.
And the children in a decade,
with a new one every year.
And then the biggest piece of all,
left us although she didn't want to.
Fought like a tiger until there was no fight left.
The original six now five,
and then things changed and
minus two like dominoes.
Don't know why we six thought
we were invincible.
Turns out not even in principle,
and then sadly one more.
Five plus one plus eight.
Too late, too sad, too much.

THE SEARCH FOR HOWLAND ISLAND

The ink is not yet dry and I have no place to lay myself down.
Stuck, sluggish, drifting, and struggling
with my old map bleeding ink.
Low clouds with heavy rain surround us.
No runway, landing lights or stars.
We are too close to the ground.
Heaven, sky and sea, all the same in the dim vastness.
There is no one to talk to,
static doesn't answer.
The folks in the tower have gone home.
Tired, tired, tired of waiting and hovering.
An ancient bird, nearly blind unable to hunt.
Patience is something I am almost out of and yet we continue…
There is just enough fuel for a few more passes.
Dodging the downdrafts, that could slam us into the waves.
And we will limp on straining,
searching almost stalling
and circling, longing to see the narrow thin strip,
of illuminating safety,
somewhere down there,
in a stormy sea of blackness.
Sky and water the same in the darkness.
Hoping someone will be there waiting for us, tending the lights.
Praying it will get better,
easier and saner when we find land, if we land.
And you ask me if I'm OK.
And I say, "Yes."

But what is my alternative in answering that question?
The only answer is "yes."
Don't ask me again.
I am not an angry adolescent railing against the world,
the sky, the fates, the unfairness of life and love
and that lack of a storybook ending.
And finally we stall, there is no more fuel.
Coasting on hope, until the engines stop
and we drop into the sea.
Straight ahead, unsteady as she goes.
One more prayer.
Is that a light through the rolling black heavens?
I think I can just make out the moon rising above Howland Island.

THE STRAY WE SAVED

He sat there like a lost and frightened child.
Mewing to the sound of passing cars,
just about to step into the street,
I snatched him up and now this cat is ours.
He purred and was content to sit and eat.
Sleeping on a lap, pillow or bed,
adopting a brownish fuzzy quilt,
mother lost, suckling on the fuzz instead.

Timid ventures up the curtains stuck,
unable to make his own way down.
As time went on his bravery increased,
so did the volume of his small meow.
His circles larger and larger then back home,
exploring the neighborhood on his own.
At dinnertime he cried outside from the windowsill,
and biting anything that crossed his path,
taking on a cat ten times his size,
his posturing and tough act made us laugh.
As he began to grow, so did his need
to bang around and knock things to the floor.

His cries insistent if he is left outside,
wanting to be sleeping in the house.

KILL THE CRITIC

That haunts your success,
And says you're not good enough?
You are plenty good.

LONELY WAVE

A wave of lonely
washes over me,
opening up a hollow
in my chest
as sand shifts
I stumble into
the wide and deep.
Flipped like a switch,
light into darkness.
Absence of air.
I cannot breathe.
The suddenness
of the deluge
caught me unaware,
and unprepared
for the pressure
my chest heaved
craving oxygen
choking on tears.

CHAPTER FOUR: BREAKTHROUGH

Winter can be interminable. Each day accommodations must be made for the cold and wet. It never seems to end. But when those first few sunny days of spring peek through the otherwise dismal landscape, everything seems to get a little better, as if given a gift of what is deserved.

The breakthrough comes when all of the uncertainty makes more sense than the pain. Breathing freer, each day feels stronger and more hopeful. Hope, indeed, becomes a word that seemed unthinkable, let alone unutterable. Someone new might appear. Joy returns in increasing measure. Going out doesn't seem monumental. Even though it may just be your perception, you might have ceased being the hot topic at playgrounds or fodder for party gossip. You might survive this divorce thing after all.

The sound coming from your mouth surprises you as a laugh, not a sob. You entertain the idea of a future of making plans, good plans for you and your mental health. Whether planning something big or small, you are doing something on your own. Doing something. The face in the mirror with the puppy dog sad eyes lightens up. Singing along with the radio is possible again. Love songs cease being repugnant. Spring has broken through and you can breathe again.

MARRIAGE INVESTMENTS

If marriage were a business,
no one would invest.
Fifty percent failure rate,
Diminishing returns.
Huge capital outlay (think in-laws)
Slow return on investment,
Second generation eating up the profits,
With no guarantee of future development.
Real estate is safer.

EVENTUALLY EVER AFTER

It's all the doing
day to day
just to get you by.
Sink full of dishes
car's in the shop
another round trip to drive.
Deadlines loom and
Headlines scream.
And I can't remember
what ever after means.

And you say softly
It's always worth the wanting
wanting something more
something beyond ourselves
something to look forward for
nothing's perfect, nothing's new
but this I know for sure
If I had my ever afters
they would be ever afters
with you.

UPSETTING THE APPLE CART

If you want to know who your friends really are,
mention you are separating from your spouse
And then be prepared to receive all the unsolicited advice
from the people who understand your situation the least—The Marrieds.
"Did you try everything?"
they will ask as if you came to this heart-wrenching reality
lightly without long agonizing thought.

"We dodged that bullet,"
they will say, laughing to one another
as if somehow that insulates them from their own marital strife.
"You should stay together for the children's sake"
because a martyr makes a great parent.
"You can't get divorced.
You are the only couple we know still married besides us,"
which is a great reason to stay together.
"Does he have someone on the side?"
they'll ask, eyes a bit too shiny and bright.
The invitations will be fewer or people will take sides
even if you and your ex-spouse don't.
And people you haven't seen much
will hear about your situation and want to know all the gory details
so the most intimate secrets of your life can be fodder for gossip
spreading like wildfire.

Some people will understand it's not about them
and rally behind you and embrace your new status
knowing that is what you need most

to be loved for you yourself alone.
And a few might say, "God give you the strength,"
and give you a hug,
which is the kindest thing of all.

A KISS TO CARRY TILL MORNING

Night is a time for darkness and shadows
Fears to grow larger and reason to wane
Wind taps the fingers of branches on windows
The comfort of silence is longed for in vain

Brief as a kiss will carry till morning
Quick as a spark as it bursts into flame
Terror surrounds real or imagined
Empty consuming this place with no name

Heartbeats as loud as a hammer to glass
Shattered and groping blood warms cold fingers
Through the window a sliver of light
Hope shines at last uneasiness lingers

Fear is at bay or just back without warning
A kiss to protect and carry till morning

ON SEX WITH THE EX

Not to berate
It wasn't great
Better just to masturbate
Keep a clean and separate slate
Just because we can
doesn't mean we should
And if I recall
It wasn't all that good
The world will have to change its course
For me to get back on that horse.

HAIKU

I dated a man
He didn't wear underwear
Nothing to pick up

MIDDLE OF THE NIGHT

I wonder if I conjured you
in the middle of the night
to soothe my lonely soul
with thoughts from long ago
When we were young
and had no responsibilities
and you smiled at me
the world was open
and I walked into your arms

And now I remember
your smooth skin brush
my lips and your arms
holding me close and I
felt safe for a moment
and then a shallow intake
of breath and my chest
again crushed by my
responsibilities

Your laugh rings in my ears
My skin tingles from a long-ago touch
And I wonder if this happiness
can be mine only
in the middle of the night
just long enough to soothe my soul
in dreams and upon waking
I face the day alone
wondering about possibilities.

CRASHING IN

I came crashing in
like an army on horseback
all hooves and breath
and heat
blood pounding
tearing at the ground.

You sat there quietly
tipped your chin and smiled
letting me know
you heard me.

I paced and flailed
and sat
blood pounding
in my ears
I took a breath
and was drawn into
the aperture
of your eyes.

SPRING

We will be together or we will not be.
What's planted will grow strong roots or lay fallow.
There will be no marker, stone or tree or vine.
Spring will come as it always does late or early.
The earth will wake and small shoots will appear,
even if the winter seems forever.
First the timid crocus or shy daffodil will rise.
Deep green young stock with purple and yellow,
petals spreading stretching out a claim.
Slowly reaching and blooming toward the sun.
Ground may crack parched in the waiting.
The dew will nourish until the water falls,
That will come late or early. It always comes.
And love strong and beautiful like the first bud,
Entwines the heart and gives reason for the beating,
Brief as a March shower just enough to wet the ground,
There will be no marker, stone or tree or vine.
Grasses will grow around the spot in summer heat,
Drying out as shadows grow shorter as the days,
Blowing gently as autumn readies the earth for sleep.
The grass will wither and join the ground readying.
For spring to come again, late or early it always comes,
and love never dies it will, late or early remain.

ON THE WIND

I looked for you
in the ancient hills of Judea
that Israel has made green.

I searched for you
in the memorials to all of the fallen
Artifacts of our ancestors.

I listened for you
in the songs of the children with voices
strong and rich with laughter.

And all along the howling winds
of old Jerusalem
Whispered your name.

SIDEWALK CHALK

Bright colors flash against the gray
The colors of the sea
Green foam lights against the white
and blue the darker depths display
Vermilion the color of the sky
When the sun sinks low and magical.
And if we could just jump and follow
Mary and Bert into the sidewalk scenery,
To the other side of light and swim
in the quiet sea and float and be.

THOUGHTS ON MASTURBATION

The best thing about masturbation
there is no need for a reservation
You know exactly what you want and need
The pressure position angle or speed
And no worry about pregnancy or STD
All that's required is time and privacy
And maybe a hot fantasy
A magazine, DVD or book?
Some mood music or the Internet.
Porn of any type or perversion.
Surf the sites whatever is working
Why should your sex life suffer?
Just because you're all alone.
A good idea? A lock on the door,
Erase the browser history before
Your teenagers see the screen.
So you don't have anything to explain.

THE WAVES

The day, the wave
Itself repeats
and out and back
empty beach then filled again.

I sit and watch and see
The full and empty
—and wonder
is this just all?

The sea takes back
what it gives out,
of waves swelling,
and then nothing.

Footprints exist so brief.
Footprints erased and yet,
they are here under waves,
to bear witness.

Long to be with me
close to me,
like the sea, to a wave
eternity.

And hold me faithful
with the steadfastness
of stone,
and the solidness
of skin.

BALLOONS

She used to love the park, the peace and quiet, when they would walk along together among the trees and flowers. Smile at the children with their shovels and pails building dreams in the sandbox. Sometimes he would push her on the swings and when she swung back close to him, he used to ask her how she felt about things. And she would become thoughtful and she used to answer him. When there were swings. But that was a long time ago. Now they are just horizontal bars decorated by an old pair of sneakers. The park mostly weeds and crabgrass and the sandbox is filled over with cement and covered with cigarette butts.

Now he mostly talked at her. And it is never quiet. He fills every inch of space with noise. He showers words over her, pouring out of him and all over her all the time. And she treads through the words like deep water trying to keep her head up above all the words. And she mostly doesn't talk or laugh or comment. She mostly just holds her breath. And the words keep coming. And here they are again at the park. A child is walking quickly with his mother. She is pulling him and he is tripping over his feet trying to keep up. He is holding a balloon the color of egg yolk. She stops to answer her phone and lets go of his hand for a moment. His hand drops to his side. He looks up into the sky and back at his yellow balloon and smiles and lets it go and smiles, watching.

His mother holds the phone away from her ear and scolds him for letting go of the balloon but he isn't listening. He is watching the balloon go higher and higher and getting farther away into the clean cool quiet air.

And she watches it too from her bench. And she imagines how wonderful it would be to be that balloon. That balloon floating higher and higher, free in the quiet looking down with no one talking at it. No sound at all, traveling wordlessly and higher than even the birds.

And he says,

"I don't think you understand the seriousness of the situation."

And she laughs. Well, not really, not at first. Really not a laugh but more like a squeak or a rusty faucet that hasn't been opened or had water run through it for a long time.

And he says it again,

"I don't think you understand the seriousness of the situation."

She takes her eyes reluctantly off the balloon so high now it's a dot of yellow in the sky, a tiny sun flying away. And she turns to him to speak and just laughs. A chuckle really, not quite a laugh, and then a chortle and then a belly laugh. She can't stop herself. She didn't mean to be rude, but her whole entire body begins shaking with mirth or madness and he stops talking just then and opens his mouth and starts filling up with air.

Like a balloon top to bottom. Just his narrow face at first, filling out nicely and then turning chubby and then his neck bulging and shoulders broad and then rounded and he begins to rise off the bench. His shirt puffs out like the marshmallow man and his tie curves like the letter *C*. His belt expands and bursts. And she arches her back and howls.

The more she laughs the more he inflates. He calls for help from inside his enormous face. Tears are streaming down her cheeks. Her shoulders heaving and still she can't help herself or him. She giggles and doubles over as he lifts into the air. His feet the size of bowling pins just out of her reach if she reached up. She sits up still holding her sides and laughing as he clears the top of the apartment house next to the park.

Something has broken free inside her. And she lets it out, laughing. And she is still laughing as he becomes a black-and-white spot in the sky. She picks herself up wipes her eyes with her sleeve and walks toward home laughing in between deep gulps of air and giggling. Really enjoying the quiet.

WITH OUR HEARTS, IT IS NOT FOR US TO SAY

With our hearts, it is not for us to say
To be blessed or cursed and wounded rightly
Love elusive as starlight in the day

It is not easy wishing love away
One never knows when it will come mightily
Love elusive as starlight in the day

It may come softly and appear to stay
Flush-colored on the pale cheek so brightly
Love elusive as starlight in the day

Heart that blinds and mind madness away
Unseen the motives darken just slightly
With our hearts, it is not for us to say

Someone unseen then enters into play
Forces of attraction tangle tightly
Love elusive as starlight in the day

And then situations alter slightly
New love befriends the heart amends rightly
With our hearts, it is not for us to say
Love elusive as starlight in the day

BASHERT

I heard you whisper, "Don't leave me"
Sitting in my red leather chair in the office
You were watching me organize
my paperwork for the trip.
Laughing I leaned down and kissed you
"I'll be back," I said, not wanting to leave.
You pulled me into your lap and held me,
and in that perfect moment you were mine.
And I wonder every time we part
the kiss good-bye a last embrace—
When you will leave me?
And I try not to plan the future
try not to dream of us together.
Explain to my heart that you are borrowed
And can never truly be mine
And the house we don't share is too quiet
And I go to sleep alone
Wanting you, missing you
Knowing that you love me
You show me every day
Maybe no one belongs to anyone
And bashert is a lie.

THE PATH

The passion and the terror hand in hand
As we walk uncharted courses deeply mined
Quietly reviewing nothing planned
A chance to rest? No place like that to find.
This road retreat is painful and apart
So we stumble lost in our own thoughts
A passion burns to finish what we start
Unseen dangers leaving us distraught
Advice given freely circles round
Together we must find our own way through
And when we surely lose our way and ground
This journey we have chosen only ours to do.

If we succeed, the pleasure and the pain
The privilege to give our love a name.

THREE MORE CANDLES

On a cake I will eat without you near
In room full of love without my love
It is not your choice and yet you choose
I spend my nights alone with the phone
cradled between my shoulder and chin
your voice in my ear so close
that I could almost touch you, almost touch
And my control and will and wants
do not make it so or any difference at all
and you not here for another celebration
to mark another occasion and I pretend
it doesn't hurt and ignore the deep sighs
that escape when I'm not vigilant and guarded
I know you want to be here and you cannot be and somehow
that makes it all the more difficult and sad and lonely
and still I tremble at the thought of you
and sigh at the loss of you and wonder
how many more nights I will be alone with you not here
Another candle? Two or three more candles?
When the spark goes out in my eyes.
When the thought of you no longer makes me tremble
Until the thought of you leaves me weeping
And broken and alone with no more candles.

GAMBLING

Never won the lottery
And never bought a ticket
Decreases the odds.

HAPPY JUST TO DANCE

Feel the music match your heart
Let the doubts fade away
I may not know all the steps
But I'm out here anyway
Happy just to dance

I didn't ask you for anything
It isn't Judgment Day
Try to reinvent your life
It's going to happen anyway
Be happy just dance

The wallowing will remain
Until you say enough
More than the sum of your pain
Rejoin the human race
Move your feet and dance

Listen to the music
Your heart used to sing
Put back as many pieces as you can
Listen hard to the subtle swing
Be happy it's your dance

COUGAR TOWN

He was twenty-nine.
"I am Mrs. Robinson."
He asked, "Who is she?"

CHAPTER FIVE: BREAK FREE

Thundering down every runway in history that has ever supported an airplane, no one inside, including the pilot, has ever believed in his or her heart that the half-million pounds of steel and bodies actually have a chance to gain altitude. When the roar turns to a faint rumble, like laughing without coughing after bronchitis, you realize that this thing might work.

Cognitive dissonance is your best friend. Your marriage was not bad because you have grown. Other good things came from it, not least of which are your children. Divorce is just one part of your life and history. A lot of people, a lot of good people, have gotten divorced and survived and prospered and been happy. It defined them, but it doesn't have to define you.

A THORN

All children want their parents to stay together
Happily ever after and riding into the sunset
Life is simpler when you stick to the script
Wishes can become dreams with work not magic
And in the real world pumpkins stay pumpkins
And a kiss doesn't magically change everything
Glass slippers shatter and the prince and princess separate
And deviate from the story line, no wicked witch needed.
Just a different twist in the plot and the story goes on.
A mouse takes a thorn out of the paw of a lion.
A tin man gets a heart, scarecrow a brain,
and the girl finds her own way home.
And happily ever after becomes the best we can.

YAWNING AND STRETCHING

Yawning and stretching,
reaching for your warm body,
matching your breathing.

Peaceful and quiet,
safe and serene for the night,
brings you in my dreams.

NOT FINISHED

You reminded me gently
with your eyes smiling
that I am not finished
being a woman.

You reminded me slowly
with your lips searching
I am still wanted
for me alone.

You reminded me keenly
with your warm touch
I am attractive
After time's ravages.

You reminded me truly
with your heart beating
that I am loved
by you alone.

NOT SO HARD TO FIND

You don't belong to me
And have never been mine
Our hearts know each other
from somewhere in time.
And knowing you're out there
At the end of the line
Means I'll never be lonely
Not so hard to find.

Our days and our nights
all mixed upside down
Somehow there's a place
where joy abounds
Maybe just a minute
or the echo of sound
Somewhere to be
not lost just found.

SOMEONE ELSE'S CHILD

Early on when we were us,
we watched a child receive her name.
She smiled up at you all pink and soft.
Your strong arms open inviting her in.
And she sat contented
in the crook of your arm.
Happy to observe the world
from her cozy perch.
And I loved you so completely then,
knowing our children would be well loved
in the safety of your arms.

E-MAIL FROM A MAN

Words on a page
Set my heart apace
with possibilities.
But are they real these words?
Not even ink, on parchment or vellum.
I cannot hold them in my hand.
They have no smell or weight.
And it frightens me how easily erased
they disappear, blotted out of existence.
As if never there at all
except for the faint beating of my heart.

HOW CAN I PRETEND?

I got the invitation in the mail,
And memorized each last detail,
A reunion of all our old friends,
I will have to make amends and miss the soiree.
I cannot pretend I do not love you.

A casual kiss on the cheek,
if you touch my hand,
my knees go weak, how will I explain
the flush on my face when I hear your name?
To look at you and fall into your deep brown eyes,
there will be no way to disguise my longing.

A MOMENT

I drop my chin into my shoulder
For the moment I cannot meet yours eyes
I have nothing to fear from your gaze
Overwhelmed by sudden intimacy
My heart stops and then beats wildly
As I raise my eyes slowly
and search to find your face.
You are smiling,
and I should have known,
for acceptance shines back at me.
From your loving eyes.

FIRST LIGHT

When you touch the match to the wick
And a small flash ignites the flame
In that tiny moment of illumination
Think of me.
And when the wax melts down
and the candle grow short
more a glow than a spark
and extinguishes itself
a whisper of smoke will escape
just before the last ember
dies away.
In that darkness
my light will still be burning
The glow always constant
The flame kindled forever
Beckoning you into the light.

HOW TO TEACH A NINE-YEAR-OLD HOW TO DRIBBLE A BASKETBALL

"It's a test and I just can't do it."
"You have to write me a note to get out of it."
This request comes from the bravest person I know, my nine-year-old.
"I can't write you a note. It's a lie," I said.
"I know, but then I won't have to do it."
"You'll still have to do it."
"I can't."
There was that word again.
"Have you learned how to in class?" I asked.
"Yes, but not enough. He spends all his time with the boys who play on his team after school and we sit on the sidelines. And when you don't do it right, he yells."
I know this teacher, I had him too a long time ago when I was nine. I didn't have the strength or power my daughter has, just the determination of a girl with brothers on either side and a need for equality. As a feminist, this didn't sit well with me, I took her out in the cold and dark in her pajamas.
"Don't slap the ball," I told her.
She bounced the ball off her shoe it rolled into a puddle now each bounce was marked by wet circles and we played. And I showed her how to dribble the ball.

"Cup your hand like you're holding an orange, keep the ball down low and start slow so you can control your forward motion."
We practiced changing hands and going around parked cars under the streetlight.
"Look at me," she yelled, delighted.
"I can do it. Watch me. I can do it."
I was not surprised. She changed hands like a pro. First right, then left and back to right. There was no moon, we couldn't see the basket so shooting wasn't possible. I told her to aim at the rim and throw it as hard as she could. It didn't matter if the ball went in or not. What was important was to make some noise. And the next day she caught me hard around the waist when she returned from school.
"Mom, Mom, Mom!" she yelled.
"I got eight and a half out of ten." I knew she could do it.
Now she knows, too.

I DREAMED OF THE HOUSE WE USED TO SHARE

I dreamed of the house we used to share,
Little shoes abandoned at the base of the stairs
Midnight wanderings and cuddling in bed
Lullabies and kisses, things left unsaid.
Halls filled laughter anger and despair.

I dreamed of the house we used to share,
Where our children crawled and said their first words.
Needs and desires spoken and unheard.
We planted trees that bore no fruit
Lived and loved and life took root.

I dreamed of the house we used to share,
The birthday cakes and entertaining.
And the food more important than the feelings.
The children grew and brought their friends,
Apologies meant nothing with no amends.

I dreamed of the house we used to share,
Another family is living there.
The anger now is so much smoke.
We began again in separate spaces,
Where trees give the fruit of hope.

IN MY DREAMS

When the solitude of night
gives way toward early morning
and darkness turns
toward the breaking
of the day.
The birds stir the air
shattering the silence
and sleep still eludes me.

Turning my pillow
to the cool side of the linen
closing the blinds against the light
closing my eyes again
I imagine you near me
reaching out I trace
the contours of your body
with my fingertips

You reach for me in slumber
and pull me closer
pressing my cheek to your shoulder
trying to match your breathing
soft, deep and even
You sigh, I breathe deep
falling into sleep
looking for you in my dreams.

MELANCHOLY HEARTS

Still all aquiver,
Am I just your violin?
All the notes are yours.

NICOLE'S HORSE

And you with such a pedigree think I am such a prize.
A broken-down old show horse too old to show.
My teeth are ground down smooth and need work.
Swayed back, saddle scared with thinning mane.
And don't get me started on the tail.
You reminded me what I was like then.
Strong, powerful and full of spirit.
When I didn't even know anyone was watching.
And once again I hold my head up and back straight.
Prancing around the ring like a young champion.
And you see me with love and light in your eyes,
and for you I am enough just the way I am.
The gate opens and you swing it back wide.
Letting me run with the sun on my back,
to graze the sweet grass in the garden.

MY ROCK?

If I am your rock,
It is because you love me
dual sanity.

SALT AND PEPPER

When the salt and pepper is more salt than pepper
when dimples become wrinkles and smile lines become maps
and large print isn't quite large enough
and we need glasses to find our glasses
We can both blame the smell and strange grumbling on the dog
and watch your children and my children make us proud
and enjoy the same joke over again, not remembering the punch line
and the little blue pill and hot flashes keep us both warm at night
and we try to figure out why we went into the kitchen
and laugh and hold each other and still feel that spark
and play with our grandchildren and teach them to think
sharing our wisdom with everyone whether they want it or not
and see the world anew and never stop learning
and celebrate a little something each and every day
feel lucky to love and to be loved and never slow down
our bodies may falter but our spirits still soar.

THE FIRST RAIN

The first rain
comes on
suddenly
I listen,
warm
from inside
watching
a window
becomes dark
with rivulets
of water
they reach
my arms
neck and heart
I close my eyes
open my mouth
and drink in
the sound
voices
of love
smiling, "Welcome home."

A DIFFERENT KIND OF GOOD-BYE

My vision is blurred. I cannot swallow the lump
lodged in my throat. My stomach hurts.
I can't seem to read further than the first two lines.
My glasses dirty with fingerprints. I take them off,
and wipe them clean with the hem of my shirt.
Still no clearer as I wipe my glasses again this time tears.

Cancer, hospice, and misdiagnosis, affairs in order.
Pain management, groggy and prepare for the worst.

My brain scrambling to make sense of the words.
My breath catches and tears fall. I cannot see anything.
And I understand too well what this news tells.
I will lose another woman I love to cancer.
Her car the one I learned to drive in,
White VW Rabbit with an easy clutch.
She made me seven-layer chocolate birthday cakes.
I never left her house without a jar of homemade jam.
Her home was where I ran to when I needed to run.
Adopted as the third sister, we all used the same fake ID.
You knew, Betty. And now none of us would be carded anymore.
There was always coffee made and something sweet to go with it.
A hug in your blue terry cloth robe at any hour,
and you understood sometimes
no words were necessary.
There was always music and laughter.
And problem-solving sessions at the table in the kitchen,
Where the chairs swiveled and elbows were permitted.
And your hair, Betty, always done,

the vague smell of cigarette smoke mixed with your perfume.
You never went gray even after we all did.
You promised us so many times to quit.
But it doesn't matter anymore.
There is barely time to say good-bye.

THE HOUSE

Over the doorstep,
I have never set foot
in the house in my mind.
And yet I have been there many times,
traced the rough hem walls with my fingers.
Padded barefoot over the smooth hardwood floor.

I have opened the windows to the clean breeze.
And seen the deep green of fir trees beyond the yard.
The rooms are few and bright and painted the colors of the sea.
The quiet undisturbed but by the clicking of keys
It is you, creating something.

The air is heady with the smell of banana bread
baking in the old black iron stove with legs.
The house is lived in.
Big overstuffed scarred leather chairs
rest by the fireplace waiting for a cold night.
But they will wait, for now it is summer

The warm afternoon light streaming in
A wine bottle sits open breathing
on the counter,
two glasses at the ready to be used
The timer chimes and you emerge
with oven mitts holding hot bread
"Welcome home"

A LATE-IN-LIFE LOVE SONG

I have been around long enough to know there is no forever.
Just because you say it, doesn't make it so.
And I will not promise you something I know can never be,
so for as long as we last, it's you and me.

You are in my heart and soul and that's how it will go.
Freedom is another thing that changes when you love,
Beholden to someone is not the same as tied down,
This is a really long way to say,
I am way more happy when you are around.

BECAUSE

Other people's plans
Will not help make you happy
You make you happy.

JUST NOT AS HUSBAND AND WIFE

Once you were my whole world
I gave up everything for you
I wanted to be your happily ever after.
You knew what you wanted
and I tagged along for the adventure.
Didn't know it would last twenty years.

I'm not angry anymore.
Useful but wasted emotion I
want only the best for you
And for the family we made
and put out into the world
We receive back tenfold
We will be grandparents together
Just not husband and wife.

LIPS

Lips swollen puckered lined,
crystals of salt left behind,
I have not been to the sea.
It's the way with you and me.
My body bathed in your breath.
Glistening, the pads of my palms
map the naked contours
of your cool, pale flesh.
Fingertips hold and skim
and roam and trace.
Never have I known a body so well
or so intimately. Muscles stretch
taut, ravenous and raw.

There is no need for make-believe games.
No striptease or delicate lace.
Leather restraints or studded collars,
Whips or knives or ties that bind,
No soft lights, candles or unchained melodies.
I see my lover's face in daylight
The first touch spreads like wildfire
Burning deep into my soul.
Trembling wanting consumed by flames.

SELF-ACCEPTANCE

Why do we remember the bad things people say?
That distort the reflection in the mirror,
Confirm the unkindness spewed and thrown away,
That we repeat to ourselves year after year.

Stuck with the sadness and dissatisfaction,
hurt and humiliated by words that shouldn't be said.
Those wounds don't belong to us until we swallow them.
And then they sit and fester and grow becoming the view.

We never chose to be what we are, genetic blueprints.
These are the only skins we will ever wear,
What matters cannot be seen from a shiny surface.
Why is that picture so much more important?

So hard on our fragile souls not being perfect,
It isn't really being at all, the search for flawless,
Starving and sweating and going under the knife,
Taking for granted the miracles of imperfection.

The imperfections that make us special, unique, human.
Refuse to carry the observations of the unkind and judgmental.
For they too carry the same hurt and humiliation,
they just don't know it, enjoy the view.

TILL DEATH

Just like it always
It is not enough reason
Why then forever?

TODAY

The good in today
Is just enough to dust off
your red party shoes

WONDERMENT

I moved away from him, away from the arms I crave.
Lifted my chin and focused on his eyes. I did not let
his handsome features distract me. I am so easily distracted.
"Did You Choose Me?"
The question like a fever had been plaguing me for days
Hotter, as harsh daylight gave way to the evening
and burning out somberly into night
Things loom so large when left to fester in dimwitted semi consciousness
In the darkness prowling down slowly into a searing tight knot

His smile was one of amusement. His head tipped to the side
His strong shoulders dipped slightly.
A small sad sigh hung between us,
That I would have to ask, that he would have to answer.
That I would need, the reassurance of words.
I am all about words. Except for when I am at a loss.
And with him, with this big huge burning love, I am.
The loving is simple, the situation is complicated.
And there are no rules. Well, none I recognize.

His face gave no clue and then he grinned like a child.
Caught up in a fib but not a big or important one. And I played along.
Watched his face for something and then the words came,
He told me a story, our story.
One of want and wonderment and of choice.

QUIET

Have you listened
to your inner voice lately?
She is very wise.

BROKEN FREE

There is no limit to the number of loves one has in a lifetime.
I have been blessed from birth with the unconditional kind.
And given birth to another kind of love. That is soft and sweet
and ever changing.
My heart has been broken and mended and broken and mended again.
Surrounded by choice, with friends and family who keep my heart safe.
And let my soul be with no bounds but bonds of loyalty and faith.
And that would have been enough for ten lifetimes and then I
was blessed again.
By you, my soul mate, my lover, my friend. And my heart is full.
And I have broken free.

ABOUT THE AUTHOR

Mendelson, who has a master's degree in creative writing and English literature, teaches Business English at Ruppin College. She has a son and a daughter, both currently serving in the Israeli Army. She and her soulmate both live in Israel.

"An outgrowth of the book's success is DivorcePoetry.com, where people can read Tamara's latest work, blog about their own experiences, and learn about Tamara's seminar schedule."

"Sensitive, real and raw, this book is the perfect medicine to heal a broken heart. Get two copies - one to give to a friend, and one to keep - to remind yourself that no matter how dark it gets, poetry will always illuminate your soul."

— Samantha Bennett, author of the bestselling *"Get It Done: From Procrastination to Creative Genius in 15 Minutes a Day"* (New World Library)

Made in the USA
San Bernardino, CA
13 October 2015